IAN GOUGE

HUMAN ARCHAEOLOGY

First published in paperback format, 2017;
published by the Author

ISBN 978-1-9997840-0-3

Other Books by Ian Gouge

Novels and Novellas

Mirrors - Paperback, 2017; Kindle, 2015

Writing to Gisella - Paperback, 2017; Kindle 2015

Losing Moby Dick - Paperback, 2017; Kindle 2015

Riding the Escalators - Paperback, 2017; Kindle 2015

The Big Frog Theory - Paperback, 2017; Kindle, 2012

Short Stories

Secrets & Wisdom - Paperback, 2017

Poetry

Human Archaeology - Paperback, 2017

Collected Poems (1979-2016) - Paperback, 2017

Second Sight - Kindle, 2013

Walking Thru Fire - Kindle 2012

Table of Contents

The Grand Tour 5

Outback Memorial 9

The Chef 10

Archaeology I 12

Archaeology II 13

Archaeology III 14

Archaeology IV 16

Murder Mystery (or Archaeology V) 17

Standing in Doorways 19

The Fog 21

Exploration 22

Terra Firma 23

Running 24

The Grain of the Wood 25

The Challenge of Politics 26

End of Term Report 28

The Patriarch 30

The Balloon 31

Gauntlet 32

Progress (or, 'On Writing Poetry') 33

The Dissemblance of Rock 34

Post Scriptum 36

Not Unlike Cleopatra 37

Echoes 38

Noise (or Between God and the Internet) 39

Relics 41

Education 43

Nostalgia in Black and White 44

War Artist 45

Uprising 46

Lake Garda 47

An Island Paradise 48

The Permanence of Shrapnel 50

Virus 52

Time and Tide 53

Love-locked 54

In Memoriam 55

Extra Time 57
Beyond the Boundary 58
Ripples 60
Perhaps 62
Amnesia 63
Rose 64
Wimbledon Routemaster 66
Guilt 67
The Album 68
Exodus 69
Assassination 70
The Revolutionary 71
Days of Tea and Backgammon 72
Camouflage 73
A Kind of Pilgrimage 74
The Northwest Passage 76
Landfall 77
Reading the Runes 79
She Reflects On Her Lover 80
The Seer 82
Wittenberg 83
The Enchanted Forest 84
Abstraction 85
Spinning Plates 86
The Aridity of a Wasteland 91
Invasion 93
Sea Traders 94
Empiricism 95
Four Books, Five Classics 96
The Superiority of Nature 97
Mirage 98
Accent 100
Poetry 101
About 'Human Archaeology' and Ian Gouge 103

The Grand Tour

Flying through a thin light-suffused mist
is the feeling of travelling across centuries,
where physical distances have evaporated
and rationality itself might only have a limited hold.
A sun of dull gold rose through tinted windows
and dawned the intimacy of waking up among strangers
and a landscape dotted with red-brick buildings
already bathed in fluorescent light and
some vague actressy notion of glamour.
Surfaces cannot be trusted amidst
the spread of modernity whose depth is hard to gauge.

This had been a preparation of sorts.

We had hoped for a blistering morning of soaring white,
yet saw paper kites wheeling against a grey polluted sky;
saw a city that is a world
less colonised, more muscular;
a warren of narrow streets through which arteries had been
forced;
an area of heavy boulevards;
a sandy waste delimited by a pale line of trees.
It seemed like grafting the geography of one city onto another;
a temple town staring frankly into the void
with an aloof and scolding memory
both of the heat and the passage of time.

The train had a romantic name, bringing us
to an almost intact medieval life full of pilgrims,
foreigners in their own land
come empty-handed into a less familiar world.

There is always dismay at the first sight of squalor;
flecks of pink in the dark oily water
plastic bags, like dead jellyfish, small imperishable memorials.
A smoky electric light wafts out
through cloying waves of jasmine
as the evening tide of worshippers sweeps along,
bathers digging at the water with folded hands.
In signs of recognition and curiosity,
tourists photograph the disarray:
the wheeling birds on the river;
a grotesque co-mingling of light and shade;
a place where people come to die.
Strong-faced ascetics watch the scene from their haunches
as the seed of something very old fertilises the present,
an old culture, decaying for centuries
like a scene out of Chaucer.

This had been a pilgrimage of sorts.

Yet there is a new tyranny of borrowed things
- bootleg educational courses and aphrodisiacs -
in an ugly new vitality.
This vision of urban apocalypse reveals
small flyblown towns with foul air,
desolate but for giant advertising boards;
two poles in a world increasingly divided.
Where society has this cloned shape,
faith functions by an internal logic
in intolerable limbo, its middle condition
a lesson in the fragility of a power
that is bound to be broken.

Spirituality and self-discovery inextricably linked,

the drama of his appearance
and the force of his gaze
betrays the intensity laying coiled within him.
He wanted desperately to be in politics,
to portray the rage of people who knew they were once something;
yet knowledge of old languages proves
an incomplete armoury against a modernity
demanding a new class of interpreters.

This had been a translation of sorts.

The city reappears from the haze,
branches casting long shadows over powder-blue walls
almost as a kind of disguise.
There is uncertainty in rural life;
people crushingly unsure of themselves
are those for whom the past was still alive
wrapped up in the perfume of worship,
the vestiges of grand culture,
and a clean denial of distinctiveness and originality.

The seasons no longer on their side.
If only some distance could be created!

He says he is looking for a way out of the nightmare of history,
retreating in the face of rough manners
and trying to salvage a sense of self.
Language was still vivid, but become jargon
in which word and meaning had parted ways,
an ill-fitting garment that muffled the voice,
an impediment to communication.
He betrays a palpable sense of despair
that this great historical event could not

simply be shrugged off as a regrettable accident,
a misadventure shrouded in mutual embarrassment.

"Here is the problem of what to do with past;
there is more to civilisation than endurance."

I was haunted by the memory of a man
using colour with a painter's confidence
yet who could not see himself from the outside
even when what mattered was the example of his life.
We lacked a shared vocabulary,
our conversation running into the dead walls
of a language that meant everything to him.

Outback Memorial

In the smothering heat of daytime,
a lattice of mangrove roots;
and farthest from the sea,
trees thin and straight and widely spaced
line rough dirt roads only passable in dry weather.
This was no place to start a family.

> For a woman of unrestrained opinions
> it was difficult to escape the lure of alcohol.

In the morning they scope the horizon
coming barefoot over the red soil to the water's edge,
their spears hand-carved from stringybark trees.
A glance seaward and a finger across the throat
takes them to their boats,
feet spread for balance, staring intently for
a great shadow in the water.

> Painting was among her many vocations;
> but their rules infringed too greatly on her freedom
> in a horror show of cultural obliteration.

Alleviating aspects of the crisis, a leaf explodes;
in moments imbued with meaning and essential purpose
a deep spiritual and cultural overlap of existence
moving to its own rhythms,
performing great deeds of creation
to set the soul on its journey.

> Taking the empty seats for a modest fee,
> they will dance for days at her funeral.

The Chef

Even though he tried to deny it,
people always assumed there was a secret,
some mysterious herb or spice
that elevated his cuisine beyond the ordinary.

"There is nothing special" he would laugh,
"I use the same ingredients as you, nothing more."

Yet how could they believe him
when their own clumsy attempts resulted
in rancid dishes that were barely edible?

And if the key were not the ingredients,
then perhaps coded recipes passed down
through generations to a chosen few?

"I have no special recipes" he said,
the humour fading in his voice.

But still they would not believe him.

So one day they set him a challenge
and provided him with a basket of goods
and left him alone in a kitchen bereft of books.

Later, when they tasted what he had made,
they were astonished.

"I just made it up," he said, fearfully;
"it seemed natural."

But they were unconvinced;
to them it seemed far from natural.

Unable to understand,
and confused by their lack of comprehension,
they branded him a Wizard
and from then on he refused to cook again.

Archaeology I

Sandwiched between a love story and some regrettable poems,
observations of lost monuments
were given via magic-lantern slideshows
by pith-helmeted Victorian gentlemen.
The era of sepia photographs and the railroad
showed them riding camels between antiquities
and - in spite of travellers carving their names into the pyramids -
how romance clung still to the decaying stones.

Their work ethic was legendary:
their systematic approach to mysteries,
how they opened up the earth, scattered dust
to find mysterious bones, artefacts of faith,
or a Pharaoh's blank cheque
to ensure the spiritual security of his empire.
Treasure uncovered was always a dangerous temptation!

Theirs was the art of digging up the past,
collecting the lost histories of
important yet neglected stories;
of knitting a patchwork of relics together,
seeing society through material evidence,
not reaching for the first available conclusion.
And though unlikely candidates for inclusion
were politely edited out of the story,
still we are not content with the archives.

Archaeology II

A synthesis of the spiritual and physical
is a story at odds with official history,
a story told in the symbolic language
that is the ancient code.
It tells of enigmatic and fantastic people,
their origins lost in the mists;
figures that defy interpretation
with elements that are not quite human
and who do not fit the mainstream perspective.
It recounts an artificial beginning from a settled stage,
a long-term project,
a pretext to raze pagan culture and
the diversity that history does not want to recognise.

Somewhere, a highly sophisticated warehouse
conceals collections in seven galleries:
"Art objects are the only remaining fragments
that do not fit into official history.
They are the keys we use to reconstruct reality."

It may still be possible to see these elements,
curious artefacts which no-one seems to notice;
manifestations that correspond to a past reality
and which offer the basis for a new history.

Archaeology III

West of the emerald green alfalfa fields
a rocky escarpment the colour of ripe wheat
and rough hills of umber blocks
disguise a huge bowl that is still being dug out.
A jagged stone wall holds back a heap of rock
and men in rusty carts that roll on rusty tracks
fill woven baskets with sand.

A bitter wind once whipped across the desert
and into courtyards and passages,
hugging the streets of a small neighbourhood
where washing hung from windows
and opportunities to fish and hunt were reduced
to dark smudges in the ever-encroaching land.

To control river traffic, Kings fortified both riverbanks
as activity ebbed and flowed with politics;
and aware of rumours about a coup,
the Official in charge of the palace
couldn't escape his old convictions -
belief in dynamic succession that once seemed simple.

He spent years preparing his final resting place,
painted green, the colour of rebirth;
a place as close as mortal remains could get
to cozying up to the big man in the great beyond.
The reliefs still have traces of paint where
the sun was carved over bodies,
the best guarantee of being reborn in the morning.
Yet the King kept his distance in the afterworld,
in death as he had in life.

Ultimately, his tomb became a shaft that plunged into darkness
and permanently severed access to the world of the living.
The irony of needing to pass through death to become immortal!

An inscribed block of white limestone
and a courtyard once forested with columns,
offer sole legacy to all this magic.
Foreign ways eroded the civilisation
and the old kingdom came to an end,
chiseled out and sanded over.

Archaeology IV

Peeling back the pavement
reveals a rich archaeological layer cake,
entire street scenes and
the ruins of an early Roman building
demolished to make way for a new basilica.
Lift the veil and poke around
to explore the city's deepest past;
a city continuously lived in and built over,
where graveyards were filled and forgotten,
tombstones broken up and reused in walls
as the next generation's vision emerged on top.
Near the resting place of choice for radicals,
there is a dark earth-line where the river once flowed.
The ruins of the city would have been very lonely.

Passing players in a long-running story
make drawings and salvage artefacts
covering the vast sweep of human history:
an expensive and rarely used pigment,
the contract for the sale of a slave girl.
Not all archaeology is under ground;
a laboratory above the museum
plays a role in the history of things.
Divested of orange high-vis and blue hard hats,
white coats rinse away clumps of
the dark mud that marks a former course,
and gently brush soil from the brows of skulls.

Murder Mystery (or Archaeology V)

Revolution made it harder to study the evidence
                and piece together an image,
a rare snapshot of everyday life.
                Connection and consequence were
shattered when the town was abandoned so completely,
                the dark and the debris
obscuring impossibly hidden doorways
                and providing camouflage
for bodies that had been buried hastily.

Excavated from an unmarked grave -
                discovered more by accident -
a set of delicate sparrow-like bones is discordant
                with a culture where
representations of women were incredibly sensual;
                faced with that, is it any wonder
he was oedipal a thousand years before Oedipus?

The best commentary is made by those who remain silent,
                those who understand their power,
are comfortable with fundamental uncertainty,
                of undertaking the responsibility
for trying to remove him from history
                and the burden they must then inherit.
His public legacy was not immune to political upheaval,
                no matter how extravagant
his indulgence in superficial display,
                of using past glories to promise future success.

Cultural traditions defined acceptable subject matter
                and his increasing desperation

reinstated older patterns of worship
                and resurfaced ancient grudges.
Subsequent revolutions ate the young
                who were sacrificed to the cause,
their art and actions the lifeblood of propaganda.

Though everything seems unfinished and open to the elements
                as they sift the rubble for clues,
archaeology retains a forensic quality,
                a discipline of process and rigour
allowing for excavations of the imagination too
                and the inevitable reprise of
patterns thought to be universal across time.

Revolution, like archaeology,
                is an act of selective story-telling,
of taking scattered evidence and organising it into narratives
                that propound the lies we chose
knowing all the broken pieces can never be put together again.

Standing in Doorways

The threshold is neither in nor out
like a mid-air coin toss
not yet heads, not yet tails,
but something other,
an indeterminate option you were never given.
It is limbo, a state of paralysis,
of not knowing;
a fulcrum where the length of levers,
the force that could be applied,
has yet to be understood.
The outcome, you might say,
is being "weighed in the balance" -
yet balance is divorced from what you feel
teetering nervously, unsure, unstable.
You stand in the doorway, not paused exactly
but knowing "in" or "out" makes all the difference:
it sets the path for your future,
closes a door on your past;
it is the coin finally coming to rest
- heads or tails - until the next time at least.

You feel as the camel must have felt
the final straw falling.

I sit inside (is that heads or tails?!)
watching from the comfort of the sofa,
seeing you, standing in the doorway,
weighing up my offer.
You are motionless, but everything moves.
The threshold is the brink,
the tipping point of all our lives.

I watch not your eyes but your feet,
waiting for the step that will betray
which way the coin has fallen.

The Fog

The world is white.
The fog suffuses a thin light
through the bedroom window
and creates an infinite potential
for mystery and secrets and adventure.
The wardrobe doors beckon!
Outside, its fence invisible,
the long garden is now unbounded,
never-ending,
as if you could step through the mist
and into a land of fantasy and wonder.

People bemoan the fog, its chill.
Perhaps all they can see is the fog itself
and not the limitless possibilities it reveals.

Exploration

It was a small undertaking by today's standards;
navigation in its infancy
spawning a new kind of exploration.
Denying any possibility of a return,
an ordinarily dependable compass took us in a circle,
charting a beautiful road through skies
an indescribable complex of colours.

A firm friend and ally to the cause of discovery,
no man in history contributed more to knowledge:
"Too many expeditions fail by arriving" he said.

Life was to prove the truth of his prediction,
stories telling of his least successful ventures;
whole villages not turning out to welcome them.

Adding a short paragraph to the story of conquest,
year by year, exploration tears away remaining mystery.

Terra Firma

There are views in this city where
people might picture a natural wonder
yet are bound fast by the invisible cords
of trade they grew into lucrative business.

Discovering a dense network of relationships,
in his mind he was following a natural trail
and spent three decades restoring its health
in an effort to turn back the clock.
Taking apart their urban places conceptually,
he stripped all features from the map
and built a landscape from the bottom up.

This was a rare glimpse of the way things used to be!
A slowly meandering stream and
beaches that ran along stretches of both coasts
described a place that didn't exist,
a place of amazing natural potential
in a city where people couldn't picture wonder.

Running

I always wanted to go to the north,
to escape rotten feudal traditions and the trivial domestic comforts
unjustified in undermining my ambitions.
Their telling us what to do only disoriented us further;
fun and leisure were remote things,
and Art seemed to belong to a fantasy world.

Education at the edge of futility force-feeds
an unstoppable stream of regurgitated detail
running as rats through the streets,
driving old and artificial names into my mind
like soldiers marching to the battlefield
in some crazed unquestioning frontline mode
not knowing that the war had ended.

Walking through bamboo forests
I wanted to be part of the new,
so I usurped tradition to become a landscape painter.

It was the first time I really used my eyes.

The Grain of the Wood

Do you see that face in the grain of the wood?
The hooked nose; the frown above bushy eyebrows?
Do you sense the menace in that warped smile?
There is witchcraft and entrapment there.
Do you see the wings of that bird,
spread wide in its swoop toward the window,
lured by sunlight and the make-believe of escape?

Perhaps.
Perhaps it is mainly children who can see these things;
innocents who see elephants and alligators in clouds
through car widows on long motorway journeys.
Is it the freedom of imagination
or the chains of boredom
that opens their eyes this way?

Do you recall the copse near the lake
where we used to stray an age ago?
And if so, can you see, etched in your mind's eye
the clumsy initials we once carved there?

Since you have been gone
I have not ventured to the lake, that copse;
but somehow, once again, I can see
monsters in the grain of the wood.

The Challenge of Politics

Intoxicated by the old way of thinking,
a dawning sense of the mission's gravity
surfaces sentiments that have bubbled under
and a fresh pessimism about our ability to shape the world.
Having lost the custom of thinking strategically
we find ourselves living in different times
and paying too high a price for the privilege.

Over-stretched from misguided zeal,
post-mortems come thick and fast
as sacred dramas pushed too far
highlight trends that cannot be explained,
and blood and treasure is wasted on
incessant grumbling against elites.
Lost in a narrative about itself,
a vision of how the world is supposed to work
becomes a tired metaphor,
a relic of the recent past,
the natural passing of a phase.

An inadequate philosophy
spawns a flimsy version of historical development
where many of the old myths have run their course,
and balance is gradually restored to
a natural turning of the historical wheel.

Yet now is a time for revolutions, not for patching;
the ripping up of consensus in
a race between education and catastrophe
where rules are unenforceable without order.
Our fate is to deal with the moving parts

of an alternative story of humanity.
In a vision bolstered by new myths,
progress could create foundations for peace
and a society governed by reason
in the slipstream of triangulation by diplomacy.
Operating in this orbit,
a new narrative could take hold;
a gift bestowed by providence
- the triumph of foresighted statecraft -
is something of a cross to bear.

Somewhere there is a future to be grasped.

End of Term Report

It was a year of unrelenting misery,
the gap between imperative and action,
between rhetoric and reality,
a desert no-man's-land.

"We face an increasingly difficult task ahead."

Vigorous and relentless assaults
undermine the prospect of accountability,
a powerful narrative of blame
chipping away at the surety of values.
Veiled in respectability,
divisive statements marked by misogyny
are simply attempts to mask past failures
and wager the future on narratives of fear.
Power at almost any cost takes us
to the darkest, most dangerous place.

We are offered betterment in exchange for freedoms:
crackdowns on dissenting voices,
suspicion against an individual,
the right to privacy unrecognised.
They argue for collective responsibility for economic ills
and neglect underlying popular anger at
ignoring the consequences of resource exploitation.

Responding to inertia and failure,
we drag drowning people out of the water.

The fruits of this new bargain
is human dignity pounded to dust.

Courageous voices are needed;
ordinary heroes who will stand up.

The Patriarch

It takes understanding and compromise
to quietly work towards goals for long enough
to ponder history and culture.
Straight, reliable and exceptionally inventive,
he was cast into a role he never anticipated,
helping people go beyond entrenched mentalities
of unconscionable misinformation and hype,
of chummy conversations in the hope of obtaining bribes,
of illegally gained, wealth-producing enterprises.

Quiet, poor and fond of martial arts,
he saw 'patriots' keeping the country safe -
then inventing dangerous new epithets.
No dealings of his were questionable;
laws were slowly being put in place,
the streets made navigable,
modern lighting keeping the city bright.

He took on a country that was lost
and carried our shadows when we refused to own them.

The Balloon

Against a uniform grey sky, a balloon
          unexpected in its redness.
Escaped from a party perhaps,
          it floats with a purpose
          seemingly ungoverned by the air,
          as if steering a course
          to where all balloons must gather.
Mesmerised, you watch it for a while
          until height and distance make it small,
          indistinct, insignificant.
Yet somewhere else, other eyes cast skyward
          see the balloon for the first time
          and contemplate its origins
          and the purpose of its journey.

Perhaps there is a secret place somewhere,
          magical, mystical,
          where all free balloons meet,
          where through the blending of their vibrant skins
          they cast an arch of multi-coloured light
          radiant across uniform grey skies.

Gauntlet

It is better to take a car
          to reach the butterfly artist's house;
better to drive quickly in order to avoid
          the squealing children playing football,
and to minimise the traffic-light intrusions of
          vendors hawking peanuts and eggs.
Walking would require you to remain
          alert to the sounds of weaponry,
the echoes of crude shotguns
          made from rusted water pipes.

Paradoxically perhaps, this land is
          a constellation of electric colours
their vibrancy captured in
          the last miniature stained-glass window
left in the neighbourhood church or
          a speckled green fish in a swirling turquoise river.
It is a country optimistically
          named from the rivers that define its borders,
the now swollen and untended arteries that remain
          the lifeblood for the forces that keep it divided,
that battle to-and-fro for
          an airport whose runway lights do not work.

Labouring prisoners, their
          hands as hard as anvils,
build roads in the hillsides, forming
          zig-zag lines stretching up terraced steps.
Drive quickly past them too
          to reach the butterfly artist's house
where colours are set free.

Progress (or, 'On Writing Poetry')

Illuminating a drama already in progress,
I do not count the years as others do;
this melody of singing and urgent whistling marking
a slow and agonising transition from the world.

As nomads living lightly on the land
my people scratch at the earth
knowing a small but critical haven would prove
their measure of wealth and well-being
while sturdier survivors dominate their territory
as the benign pageant of life swirls around them.

Clouds boil up from ruined volcanoes,
grass turns the colour of toast and crackles underfoot
against the constant thudding rhythm of muscular women
venturing into a primitive world beset by new problems,
a wilderness washed by a rising sea of humanity.

Across the way a cell phone goes off unexpectedly.

Seeking a positive alternative to failed approaches
it may yet be necessary to build fences
in the places where the land runs on forever.
Striving for a vision that even a sceptic could love,
I wander like a blind man feeling his way.

The Dissemblance of Rock

We came here once and marvelled at the falls:
violence in the torrent, stillness in the pools.
Powered by recent rain, mist rose in a cloud before us
and made me - in our hand-holding - blissfully damp.

You had said something, your face serious
with that look you reserved for profound moments;
but I could not hear you above the roar,
and your words were carried away,
become residual echoes for others in the downstream eddies.

You were quiet then,
even when I slipped on the wet rock, your hand instinctively there.
Calamity averted.

I had always seen myself as the solid one,
defined like the rock, impervious, constant.
Water seemed to fit you better;
the soft mystery of the fret,
the moods of torrent and stillness,
and sometimes even a roar that drowned all things.

So what did I miss?

Now I am here alone.
There is still the rock, the water, the unquenchable noise.
Is that where I slipped and you saved me?

Imperceptibly, the rock is smaller now,
eroded by the incessant water, interminably assaulted.
And I am invisibly diminished too,

worn away a little,
my ultimately flimsy exterior lacking any adequate defence.

35

Post Scriptum

Through the smoke came voices that sounded Edwardian,
late night discussions featuring talking heads
and topical subjects that mattered to people:
moral and political realities;
freedom and its betrayal;
the architecture of happiness.

Philosophy in mainstream culture
was once a connection between television and the university.

Now something fundamental has changed,
reported outside the obituary pages:
a narrowing of the discipline;
publishing become precarious;
academics marginalised when rethinking life and death.

Philosophy has vanished.
The border guards have changed.

Wear a black armband for the era that has passed.

Not Unlike Cleopatra

Buried in a tumbledown temple
avoiding the unsentimental recycling of building stones
and overseen by a towering lighthouse,
this was a place more 'spiritual' than 'downtown'.
Manifestations of the great goddess
may lie outside the walls of the temple
amid the broken heads of statues
for there is no reliable depiction of her face.
Some fragments betray the ghostly outlines
of ritual acts of deep significance,
yet the poverty of salvaged material
obscured in a fog of fiction
makes her slave to propaganda and centuries of bias.

They praised her allure, not her looks.
Like a caffeinated burst of activity,
interaction with her was captivating,
so modern in its contradictions;
her tongue, like a many-stringed instrument,
the very wellspring of her vitality.

Today, immortalised by gaudy slot machines,
there remains perhaps an inkling of eternity.

Echoes

With no pills to drive me to sleep
I learned abandonment in strange hotels
greeting the early morning light,
purple in winter (pink in summer).
So I could absorb more of each place,
I tried to marvel at the iron bridge,
to speak English and not think in a foreign language,
sat at cafe corner tables just abandoned.
Walking through history in a stealthy but solitary line,
I sensed ghostly footsteps on the treads
their secrets almost visible in living colour,
growing deeper the longer we were away.
They are a lifeline to a world I too often leave behind.

Noise (or Between God and the Internet)

Imagine a vast ocean of mirror-still translucent turquoise
      so clear that you can see its floor,
      so vast that its shores are become horizon.
Imagine that.

One day, from an invisible somewhere, a pebble
      is dropped into the very centre of the ocean
      and a single ripple forms.
All around the ocean's edge
      people watch in awe as the simple wave
      glides silently towards them.
Imagine that.

And then, invisible to each other,
      two people (or twelve people) find stones of their own
      and toss them gently into the water.
Others watch as multiple ripples now expand, intersect,
      creating complex and wondrous patterns
      on the gently undulating surface of the ocean.
They are besotted by the magic of movement,
      of the motion they have created by their own hands
      in the simple act of throwing stones.
Imagine that.

Soon everyone has found a stone
      and the surface of the water is bombarded
      with the volleys of the masses.
Everyone needs to make their mark,
      to influence the pattern of the seas,
      and ever larger stones are thrown harder, further.
And what was once a mirror-still surface

moves beyond undulation into chaos,
        its turbulence so great that ripples cease to form at all.
And where once the sea was clear and turquoise blue,
        it is opaque and grey and chill,
        and nothing can be seen beneath it.
Imagine that.

Relics

I

Touch it gently if you must for it is a relic of the past.
Don gloves to protect it from the imprint of your fingers
and the contamination of the present
for this is History.

Once, through that window, you might have seen
the end of an era, perhaps; or on the lawns beyond,
Ladies marvelling at the majestic fountain,
its marble rumoured to have been hewn in Tuscany.

We may not know when this frame
was closed upon the world,
broken and giving way to time;
yet that which was once a poor repair
is now itself become an artefact of the past.
Touch it gently if you must.

II

Touch it gently if you must for it will be gone soon after,
imprisoned on the journey from the tangible.

Once you might have stood
('in the moment', by modern idiom)
and thought of now - today, tomorrow -
and a present so easily become the past.
Living exposes the lie of 'once',
for 'once' is now and never and always.
Examine memories as you do this ancient window;

marvel at their legacy, and how they
- like you - have travelled through time
from 'once' to 'once upon a time'…

Take care of your history
for when you are no more
who will there be to bring it back to life,
a relic crumbled into oblivion with your passing?

Touch it gently if you must.

Education

The spaces dedicated to home
are closest to the source
of cultured human cells.

Here, a few hours' effort triggers learning,
initiates steps in development;
currents flow along their wires and into
classrooms like the insides of microwaves,
devices that produce unseen heat,
cooking the brain
in the frequency window that nature uses.

Accept that children are not little adults,
can be made to break apart.
Accept that agents can harm,
intrusive thoughts revealing contentious themes.

Nostalgia in Black and White

She was good at remembering old movies,
at staring down a gun and pleading for a cigarette
with no way to tell which way it would go.

Sometimes we remembered being happy
and the testing questions to figure out who we were -
pasts so unbelievable
we needed a witness for our memories,
window boxes filled with rotting carnations.

Solitary now, avoiding even basic upkeep,
in fear of arbitrary self-inflicted punishment.
I could live another's life in the soundtrack's music.

War Artist

Caught up in a larger drama
it was a cruel adventure,
their faithful fingers depicting scenes,
recording images in the midst of battle,
identifying a war's focal point.
Vigilant during the day,
they shared the soldiers' fare
always trusting in lead and knowing
important events or battles could not be rushed.
More literary than journalistic,
fidelity to fact was the first thing -
yet they still altered drawings to make them more stirring.

Seeing exhausted horses dragging buckled artillery carts,
he wrote on the back of his sketch
"Retreat is too weak a term to use".
It was an emotional and symbolic coda,
watching people returning to peaceful living.

Uprising

The foreign press was a nuisance
with their perception of imminent crises,
making allegations of underground networks
and validating conspiracy theories -
"Merely sensible, legitimate criticism!"
- a lightning rod for a stormy mood.

His was a cavalier approach to coups d'état,
fabricating past corruption and mismanagement
in order to silence the opposition.

In a struggle over power in its most brutal form,
he was assassinated in his own offices.

Lake Garda

In appeasement towards a private war,
an unobtrusive state supervision
accepted them as worthy participants
though the majority opted for neither side.

Five days after the truce was signed
military leaders cravenly fled east
renouncing their nation without warning to its civilians.
Yet the killings did not stop with the formal peace.
Some urged a more effective and ruthless rule:
mechanised imperial slaughter;
natural caverns in the rugged country
where people were thrown to their death.

Now sites of memory merge politics and the personal
into a living history framed by ideology and sex,
even though the lovers seldom saw each other.
Nostalgia remains for anyone wishing to savour history
though three memory days is not many,
enough to expose silences and limitations,
a tangled and unsatisfactory recall of participation.

Current academic work, critical of their country,
preaches an equality of morality,
however ambiguous may be their legacy;
and in anodyne theatrical versions
carrying their own populist avoidance,
rival interpretations of events still linger.

An Island Paradise

Sunrise fills the deep coastal valley
as dawn touches the edge of the sea,
and to echoes of the pure voice of the Pacific
a slender monument casts a big shadow.
In a society still beyond our reach,
you can feel the familiarity and warmth
of chanting men and sinuous women,
and be reinvigorated by their sense of identity.

A renowned seaman and veteran,
rumoured to be there at the beginning,
is a navigator of the islands overdue for return.
From a family of missionaries and planters,
never write him off as a dreamer;
voyaging and navigation grew up around them all.

A modest embodiment of cultural revival
is the systematic passing on of language
(they have a lovely word for 'Elder')
and the way they see their place in society;
their part in a creation mythology
were values that translated into land.
There is a way of praising a sunset too,
and ancient methods of reading stars exist,
tradition still alive in the rural areas;
the greeting of teachers - the appeal for wisdom
lasting long after classes are under way! -
partly prayer and partly dramatic proclamation.

When cultural suppression was formalised
they prepared for the future by perpetrating history

in an art form that retold the past
and was instrumental in reviving interest
in the importance of traditional sacred sites.
Theirs is a culture that has survived against all the odds
though the essence of place remains elusive.
To prevent further dilution no-one visits unannounced.

Pressured by commercial interests,
businessmen overthrew the monarchy,
and now an angry outpouring of political activism
seeks a simple solution for a complex problem.

The Permanence of Shrapnel

There is a photograph of the house in
                    an aerial view of an estuary,
and on the glass that frames it
                    smudge marks left by museum goers
who have pointed out his former home.

Perhaps reverence comes from knowing
                    genius is so elusive;
rare enough to warrant understanding, investigation.
                    Research triggers ethical concerns
amid the experiments, dissections, and the genesis of
                    an array of singular medical specimens.
It is a kind of archaeology where
                    ideas and insights are kindled,
where suggestions and notions fall
                    below the common standard
that might have been expected, considering.

Ignoring vague hypotheses, for him
                    clarity would arise at unexpected times,
the happiest of accidents where
                    promise and opportunity collide
and lead him beyond the confines of his study
                    to words he had no intention of playing
suddenly dredged from the estuary's silt almost,
                    cloaked in layers of muck and magic,
whose smoothing and polishing
                    unravelled complex and mythical qualities.

Yet still he feels like a hopeless casualty,
                    the wounding bullet still in place,

his attempts to self-medicate

                    wedded to the verdict of history

and the smudge marks on a photograph's frame.

Virus

Communities think they understand,
interrogating a highly evolved spirit
to discover the root cause
of a fatigue and pain that goes unnamed
and walks around undiagnosed.

Over decades and in each generation,
an initial dormant period
creates a secret epidemic
waiting for an opportunity to launch.
Insights mark them as invaders;
abundance acting as a trigger,
their effectiveness comes from hiding in the shadows.
Awoken, delusional and crazy,
they twist and spin like drills
committing their mayhem unchecked,
taking advantage of the chaos
to successfully wear you down;
feelings of guilt, fear and shame
adding to the burden on your system.

You must understand the cause of your suffering
to return to a normal state.

Time and Tide

It had been a day of silk;
warm, still,
the water gently ruffled
to catch the highlights of a sun
dancing on the smallest breakers.
A day to walk barefoot,
sand and sea caressing;
and in the distance
the shimmered horizon suggesting
a future with edges blurred,
soft, made comfortable,
as if everything could be looked forward to.

In this light, this mood,
the inactive lighthouse
could only be romantic.

They walked as if the only things that mattered
were the sea, the sand, and their memories.
They blended smiles, matched steps,
and forgot storm-lashed days
that were wild, raw and unforgiving,
even as they forgot a future
towards which they sauntered
momentarily oblivious.

Love-locked

They are clamped to the ancient bridge defiantly,
not simply declarations that glitter when the sun shines,
but challengingly, almost demanding you admit your disbelief.

Around them, felt-pen graffitied into the ochre lime,
hearts writ large by those who came unprepared,
bereft of gold or silver embrace.
They too felt the need to make their mark.

And as I hold your hand
I see in one rough-drawn heart
a name crossed out, replaced with another.
What if theirs had been a padlocked declaration
rather than budget love,
the key thrown into the river below?

Ah, the constancy of love!
And the flexibility of the pen over hard unyielding metal.

In Memoriam

As if it were conferring some kind of honour,
they said you had been buried in the most shaded corner,
near the shattered remains of the old beech tree
felled by last winter's storms;
then they checked their records to be sure,
dusty files in dusty drawers.

Had it been so long?

As I walked towards you, pulling my scarf tight about my neck,
I wondered how recent an arrival needed to be
to remain fresh in their minds -
and wondered how much time had spent
since anyone had visited your grave.

I passed fallen crosses and monuments
- were these storm casualties too
or victims of mindless vandalism,
bullies picking on those that cannot fight back? -
and into air that seemed to darken as I neared you,
a corner less shaded than dwarfed by a clutch of oaks
that seemed to suck at both light and life.
The grass looked malnourished, vulnerable,
as if a single footfall might etch a path for all eternity.
It was a desolate, lonely spot,
even if your headstone was one of many;
a crowd of strangers brought together on a false pretext,
as if they had been cheated in some pyramid selling deal
and become resolutely silent, not trusting
any of their neighbours in case they were the perpetrator.
At least your stone was upright

even if the small chalice was bereft of use
and ivy - straying from the oaks -
had begun to encroach on your engraving.
I leant forwards and tugged at it as if
freeing your name to the miserable light
might bestow some crumb of comfort.

As I eased the carnation from my lapel
the wind tugged at my scarf
and challenged me to remain.

It was the bitter wind that watered my eye,
for I had decided I would not weep.
Yet even so, as I placed my flower
in that no longer redundant vase,
I felt the echo of the past and hoped
others might still come to remember you.

Extra Time

Later, when we searched your room -
dust from freshly-drawn faded curtains
flying abundant in the air as if
independent beings with minds of their own -
we found the sports things of your youth
hidden in a corner behind a trunk,
its leather cracked and worn.
It too had seen better days.
Too pliable to be of use now,
the strings of your racquets were soft
belying the past they must have shared;
you - red-faced, enthusiastic -
chasing down the ball cross-court
to drive a winner down the line
and shout "Advantage!".
I swear I caught a glimpse
in Uncle's normally unwavering eye
the beginning of a tear
waved away with a complaint about the dust
and how you never kept things clean.
Perhaps he knew you better than I;
brother first, father later.
If so, I did not mind.
My memories were elsewhere,
not confined to a room of ancient things
smothered by the dust of years
or the chill illumination from
a sudden winter light.

Beyond the Boundary

If they had known each other at all
we might imagine them beneath an English sun
in whites and caps and frowns of concentration,
summer birdsong punctuated by willow on leather
and spectators' gentle applause.

Perhaps one - strong-armed, accurate,
by profession an architect (the one who designed
that new library on the High Street perhaps?) - was a bowler,
able to fizz the ball in from the field,
preventing runs, tying down the opposition.
The other, burley and squat - easy to imagine
in his butcher's apron, cleaver in hand,
shaping the choicest cuts - belied physique
with a stroke that defined elegance.
He built the score, the platform for victory.

Aside from imagination, their acquaintance is uncertain,
both on the cricket field or regimented on foreign soil
where chaos and not elegance abounds;
where leather balls are become grenades;
a scamper to crease, the dash for the next trench;
where 'volley' and 'stumps' have the blackest hues;
and where there is no right way to win -
if there is a way to win at all.

There would have been a simple joy
in picnicking beyond the boundary rope,
watching them play.
Amidst the echoes of past applause,
wandering now the square that has not

been mown these past three years,
families fall into the chasm between remembrance and forgetting;
a slow bleed on shortening breath
as they learn to expect less,
and grieve the loss of the quickened pulse
and the excitements of what might have been.

Ripples

We used to fish in the summer,
hand-held lines disappearing into the rippling lake
invisible after the first foot or so.
We kid ourselves still about the blueness of water
and the perfection of the sky,
but on some unblemished days you could
pick out the ribs of the boat from the shore cafe
where our parents took tea and scones, and combined
protection with the indulgence of our freedom.
Once Jack caught a small silver fish
and we argued over its name
waiting too long to return it to the water,
disappointing the girls with its needless demise.
If there were accidents, I do not recall them now.
I remember laughter and boisterousness,
and once losing an oar over the side,
the boat rocking wildly and generating
fear and fun in equal measure.
If our parents noticed they never said,
rather choosing to softly lecture us on safety
and offer mild admonishment if more than five of us
went out at any one time.
I blur those days now into a single image
- of Jack holding up the fish, the girls laughing,
and somewhere in the bow, me intent on my line
and staring through the water -
an image that has become a photograph,
something stored in my mind to represent
childhood and how it is supposed to be idyllic.

It would be good to go fishing on the lake again,
but we would need two boats now
even though Jack's no longer with us;
his summers numbered all too few
and can only live on in our memory of them.

Perhaps

The last time he had seen her
had been on Waterloo Bridge,
collars up against an autumn chill,
pretending the after-theatre glow
was enough to keep them warm.
Had it been an insignificance
that sparked the disagreement?
Surely so.
Perhaps the wind had been too harsh,
the theatre glow too cool;
perhaps there had been a fissure
contrary, dangerous, invisible,
like a current in the Thames below.
Could he perhaps recall a jarring chill,
an abruptness in her voice,
a coldness in her eyes?
Perhaps there had been a tone,
a hint, a note, a colour.
Perhaps.
Red. Her coat had been red.
He had complimented her shoes,
her elegance, the way she wore her hair.
No blame there. No blame there.
Looking down into his open palm,
he feels again that night's cold
captured in a red coat button,
her only legacy to him
unwillingly gifted as she ran away in tears.

Amnesia

Her memory flowed like a movie,
tragedies and humiliations etched most sharply
in the exaggerations our mind creates
during the magic of turning perceptions into memory.
Experiencing the residue of promise or fate,
her extraordinary obsession with her past
was like stepping into a time machine.

But now, trapped in the limbo of an eternal present,
living under a narrow spotlight surrounded by darkness,
every lost thought seems less like a casual slip
and more like droplets of life that immediately evaporate,
fallen completely out of time.
All that lost knowledge was once at her fingertips,
like a culture before the advent of books.

Rose

Perhaps I should have brought flowers.
It would have been thoughtful; appropriate.
If nothing else, it would have allowed me to play
that pun you must have heard a million times:
"A rose for a Rose!".

Not looking with my eyes
I managed to miss how fragile you were,
blindly focussing on my own good fortune.

There were questions I should have asked -
not to you perhaps, but about you.
Like "why?'.
Why had you taken such a chance
- an anonymous lonely hearts ad -
to meet someone? To meet me?
Where was the need for that?
Not in your slimness, your blonde hair,
eyes that seemed - just once or twice - to dance.
Not in your laughter, your smile,
the clothes you wore, the things you said.
If not there, then where?

Perhaps, in a way, I did have some sense of it;
keeping my distance, a physical gap between us.
And as much as I wanted to,
I never tried to bridge that space
as we sat on the settee drinking coffee
and listening to no music.

If I had taken flowers, if I had made that joke,

if I had reached across to you that evening,
where would we be today?
Would you - like some brittle petal - have just folded,
crushed in my hands,
or would you have blossomed?

Yesterday I saw you getting petrol at the supermarket.
You looked drawn, a shadow, a fading bloom
daunted by the coming of autumn.

In the cocktail of failure and hindsight you learn lessons.
Perhaps I should have brought flowers.

Wimbledon Routemaster

If I missed - I surely did - your obvious shock
At my positively looking towards wedlock,
I have not failed to miss it since, replayed as it always is
In a monochrome excerpt etched in memory.

It was made - crossing the river - in innocence,
Casually, and without thought of consequence;
As if unwed I might be negligent, remiss,
Empty, hollow, a shadow of what I could be.

With all our shared history - and the twisted wreck
Of a persistent inability to make you mine -
Might I not for one brief moment have thought to check
If winning you might not just be a subtle trick of time?
If your unstated assumption was one day we'd be together,
Might my declaration not have been less chatter and more dagger?

Guilt

Even though it was an age ago
that image still haunts me
as if I might reach out and touch it,
a scene running on an infinite loop
daring me to do something differently.
In my dreams I do not make you cry.

I retrace that painful evening;
the slow walk up the hill where
our footsteps should have faltered
on the pavements of a crumbling world,
shocked and shaking
by an earthquake of my making.
And even though I had my reasons
to seek some distance from you,
even though you may have understood
- and then found a way
to offer me the space to work things through -
in spite of that I shared nothing,
abandoning you in the frigid vacuum
only silence can create.

In my dreams I face my fear.
In my dreams I talk to you.
In my dreams I do not make you cry.

The Album

I tried to rearrange the pattern, to shift the shapes, restart the
sequence.
I tried to alter the events but was caught in a recurring dream
      where variation and escape were impossible.
I tried to imagine a different me making different decisions.
I tried to envisage other outcomes, ones I wanted,
      ones where you were still with me.

And in the face of loss, of unwanted certainty
      I find myself immobile, disabled;
            a singer without a voice,
            a painter without a brush,
            a musician without their instrument.

The pictures I have in my head remain
      but they are fading now,
      their edges curled and torn by too frequent handling.
I should have secured them somewhere,
      created an album to keep them safe;
      but that would have deprived me the eternal futility
      of trying to rearrange the pattern into a different outcome.

Exodus

In the beginning, their search for spiritual wisdom
offered a chance to escape,
and people began to migrate to other places,
to entertain their own ideas,
to separate in order to survive.
They falsely believed they were ready
to pass on their ancestral wisdom
and fulfil their sacred obligations.

"Thoughts can penetrate the child," they said,
"and transmit the true memory of past events."

But capacities had been removed from them,
and just one small portion of their total knowledge
remained preserved in the temples:
the Stream from Heaven,
created quickly and in perfect form.

Truth was disguised in impenetrable rituals,
and events kept in their memories
- of any actions noble or great -
were just the old myths concerning the old world.

Destitute of letters and education,
warfare led to the destruction of their civilisation;
the memories of those who survived
frail doors which they hoped could be opened later.

Assassination

From the back rooms of cheap boarding houses
small and grimy windows reveal nothing but
rusted rails emerging from grassy margins
and rosebuds faded to rusty orange.
Marooned in a bleak urban landscape,
the result of domestic politics gone badly awry
are lives stunted by persecution and secrecy.

Even as their exodus unfolded
people waxed mystical about a revolution
that stood for the liberty of freedom.

Human connection on a vast scale
claimed him as a kindred soul:
"On many levels I know what freedom is," he said.

Years later, a bomb was primed for its inevitable explosion.

In the fight for places in the front ranks of the mourners
we discover how much his spirit pervades
the remnants of lives as complex as the machine of history.

He knew lines made of laws could be erased;
that the most impassable barriers were formed of words.

The Revolutionary

Some said he was a liar, an upstart and a traitor;
avoiding conflict and shunning engagement.
To others, controversial and heroic;
refusing to stand aside when others were dying
to protect the freedoms they all enjoyed.
And even when life outside became a blur
he had a way of seeing things, suddenly,
familiar sources of violence and conflict
never taking the edge off his disappointment.

Smiling valiantly, sadness in his eyes,
he was no longer condemned as a renegade before he died.

It happened
                    and then there was silence.

Days of Tea and Backgammon

War fell on them guillotine-swift, apocalyptic,
as if the world was actually finished.
Bombs, their own single nation, fell without discrimination
until silence ruled the wasteland outside the city.
Amidst thin olive trees, green like the uniforms of soldiers,
refugees lay over the country like a flood
all the world's pity could drown in.

The morning she walked out to die,
she dressed carelessly in a loose t-shirt and jeans,
each step now a painful act of will.
Their house had become besieged by silence.
Trading her body in a mould-streaked bedroom,
recognition carried mutual horror and
the shared language of dispossession,
her expression blank with practiced appeal.
Bruised from blind collisions,
she refused to accept the standard equation
and became suspicious of sympathy,
her small hands waving, weaving stories.
Astonished at the sound pouring out of her,
she discovered even grief can become a habit.

Still dreaming of marble archways and high-end stores,
women stopped living, and became ghostly
like the birds now only a darkening blur or
the multitude of souls cast carelessly onto a roulette wheel.
Some questions cannot be answered
on the long road to failure,
and when running is the only option left,
long gone are the days of tea and backgammon.

Camouflage

I looked for you in all the usual places,
yet even in my memory I failed to find you
as if you had deleted yourself from my history.
I knew you were there, somewhere;
pursuing another dream;
revelling in isolation.

"Anonymous is not invisible" you once said
as I struggled with your life,
your way of not living.

And taking you at your word
I look for you on street corners, in coffee shops;
I glimpse a hint of your smile in others' faces.
I look over my shoulder,
unable to dispel the sense that your new project
is simply
                you
                        watching
                                me.

I have never wanted to be absent, to disappear;
I have always felt that proof of life
is to make a mark, however small.
Yet here you are - or here you aren't -
making your own kind of mark
in your own intangible way,
invisible but not anonymous.

A Kind of Pilgrimage

His memoirs brim with a flavour of the time;
a bearded scholar with penetrating eyes,
he is famous in his own hometown
and leads discussions on mystic subjects,
his deep voice challenging the silence.
Wrapped to veil all but his eyes
he tours the capital under royal protection
with a broadsword in a dusty red scabbard
and attendants armed with daggers sheathed in gold.
For a handsome man wearing dirty shoes
he had little stomach for sea travel
nor for crossing a line he had scratched in the sand.

When all their ships had been destroyed by local revolt,
sea captains fanned their wanderlust
by finding water where they could.
In the thickening clouds that flooded the valley
theirs was a journey of hazard and hardship,
the line of beasts tethered head to tail
like a vast city on the move;
and as landmarks slipped beneath their magic carpets,
local guardians assigned them places to sleep
in ports steeped in many cultures.
Provisioned with cakes and silver coins,
there were banquets with turbaned sultans and mirages,
and their women, wrapped in rainbows of calico,
took their rest walking the narrow cozy streets.

Flowing like the waves of the sea,
reality lay beyond the grasp of intellect,
imprinted in rock revered by many faiths,

dwelling in cemeteries that border the coast
Death's messenger having risen against the city.
Corpses arrived on the roofs of taxis,
and something man had fashioned to measure his progress
- hand-sculptured like some gingerbread castle -
one of the Seven Wonders is already faded into ruin,
nothing left except a few scattered bricks.

Sounds of saws and hammers echo through palm groves,
and gleaming with the flash of lightning
wooden giants still creak and groan
to greet the stars on some remote mountain top,
to seek spiritual shelter amid pious throngs,
to dine with kings or share a crust.
Against the cadent spell of flute and drums,
the amber sun scours last shadows from sand-blown footprints
as the oasis disappears under a dune horizon.

The Northwest Passage

Motivated by power and prestige,
the lure and myth of the frozen north promised them
kingdoms where materials could be found and traded.
A surplus of naval officers set the position of their ships
- in a display of soft power! -
to harass foreign competition in the search for gold
and steal profits from routes already charted.

It was a long, dangerous and dispiriting search
even for men not keen to understand local cultures;
men who were happy to live on the edge,
making it up as they went along.
They had learnt to live off the land
and not to take the word of savages who had
resisted more civilised forms of exploration.

Embedded with rich cultural meaning and indigenous history,
archaeology promises to fill gaps in knowledge,
and failure - not establishing a pattern from the past -
shapes cartographic imaginations to illustrate their ideas in maps.

Landfall

There was great danger along the river
as they steered their boats
following some faint trail
to chance upon a strange coast
where the midnight sun was dying hard
and arctic air quickened the blood.
No respite was permitted until dawn.

Founding a city and marrying into royal houses,
he built on his ancestral ties while
she shone like the moon at night,
like a pearl in the mire.
Arm-in-arm their toasts to peace
advanced learning and literature,
a civilising influence arriving too late
for objectors serving their out term.
Still summoned by a sense of glory,
he raised stones in memory to himself,
bequeathing thousand-year-old sentinels
that reached to the end of the world.

Beyond this splendour lay a fearful nether world
and the anxious murmurs of a land tormented,
its earth black with human detritus.
Across history darkened by years of occupation,
flickering tapers suffuse an aura of sadness
as the old cry for peace rings out.
It is the stone of the heart, the tears of the tree;
a ruined city of hills.

In a grassy boulder-strewn glade

a slumbering emptiness of meadowland
still casts its magic of warmth and beauty.
Back in the mainstream
and merely part of the overall pattern,
we are still finding new passages.

Reading the Runes

A skein of streams sweep icily into the river
as we shiver in the streets waiting,
bloodied survivors of a costly raid
crushing local resistance and stealing the land.
The smoky haze rising beyond the Town Hall
marks a low makeshift burial mound
and centuries of kingly ambition;
a weakness for beautiful things,
glazed plates, swathes of silk,
and tally sticks for tracking trade.
In the oppressive halls of the lords,
fire seethes from flaming torches as
warriors live on in invented lands,
in chains of hill forts vying for power
and fleets that carry death and destruction.

Developing a scientific approach,
new studies reveal an image of how
a society was gradually taking shape.
They tell tales of traders
and reveal the importance of slavery,
of finer things from foreign cultures,
and the romance of those who built the great ships.
Men and women alike celebrated and traded and fought,
in the enduring spirit of an age,
still slaves to the darkest of all world myths.

She Reflects On Her Lover

He has given me an ancient silver coin
        that will one day be priceless.
It is the habit of a dreamer
        who interprets what cannot be seen;
the landscape gardener who, when hedges fall,
        sees a new landscape emerge.
Yet part of his being is already turned away,
        haunted by both past and present;
betrayal and joy keeps him awake,
        the grief of too much knowledge,
the retrospective horror of having stayed too long.

Once he lost a lover in the waves.
        My beloved is grounded in death and loss.

I have tried to turn my life into a reality
        not often within reach at my age;
it is a fearful journey into the unknown
        - nothing has ever scared me as much.
Must I expose myself to social activities,
        to living in the public view?
Others are dancing with name tags on, full-fleshed females
        gyrating against a background of black wood.
Always good at making the wrong decisions,
        I have spent the present of my life reclaiming its past.
There are glazed rose petals for dessert;
        I'll eat them in my dreams.

*

A year ago she lost her voice in a day of dreaming,

and discovered in living life in slow motion
consensus was dissolved by the implicitly unsaid
upon which they once built their narratives.
Anxiety arose from loss and separation,
past rites interfering with a future state
that exposes a heart which can be wounded.

Yet, all excited, they were still asking: "What happens next?"

*

Dissecting like an anthropologist,
absorbed in their story as myth,
we receive a letter for the dead,
a seedy side effect of expedient marketing.

Unity between thought and action, dream and reality,
in the end is too claustrophobic,
leaving no room for the symbolic.

The Seer

An imperial figure, the equal of emperors,
he felt broken and dejected,
the strain of being a mouthpiece for power,
expected to have all the elements.
Dedicated to explaining philosophy,
his decisions were based on faith.
Four generations from one family
instantly able to read the symbols;
the first of thousands of messages
was the activation of his immunity.

A promise of cures and conversions
is the touchstone of our longing.
A universal symbol of suffering and remembrance
is a bomb in a bouquet of flowers,
blood running all over like rivers
testing the integrity of the soul.

Isolated or forgotten, clues about life are elusive.
Scholars must take what they can
when life is picked up from hearsay.

Wittenberg

Squabbling over territory and influence,
the mutual intolerance of factions
obstructed the purchase of an indulgence.

In bemusing arguments,
gifted and disputatious academics
begged the right to individual conscience;

and a theological earthquake made it possible
to shout of the awakening,
a time to trigger the perfect storm.

The invention of printing press vernacular
helped standardise the language;
the growth of literacy nourishing debate.

On the south door of a parish church, a notice,
significant because of all that flowed from it,
the explosion of information, knowledge and ideas;

and though a poisonous legacy would resonate,
the right to question and reject authority
was the beginning of the end of empire.

People flocked to the new brand,
the disenfranchised making their voices heard;
a culture that encouraged buccaneers, pioneers and adventurers.

The Enchanted Forest

From the spidery script of an 17th-century account,
a Hermit used to nudge along a tale,
an ancient story re-told in many cultures.
Then plague closed the universities
and needing to inspire not just through language
they found memories were collective:
"Memories, embodying belief, marking sorrow,
are reveries crystallised in time".
Watch a tree mark the seasons;
fully dressed for summer,
it understood it needed to be around.
"The tree holds the life of the city."

Forests are inhabited by fantasy and fears,
by fable and legend and 'once upon a time'.
Some stories are beyond eloquent.

Abstraction

Romance is an overlay on reality;
rose-coloured glasses that filter
what we choose not to see.
What is the past but history
become an abstract we cannot trust?
There can be no history without romance;
the Emperor's new clothes.

We are seduced by facades;
we swallow draughts of romance
and pretend to know the past;
we look at the remarkable and miss the profound;
we take photograph after photograph,
yet capture nothing,
merely applying another coat of varnish
that keeps us from the past
 - or protects the past from us.

"Sometimes," said the Photographer,
"I don't take the shot
because the moment is what's important,
and how can you capture that?"

True history resides in all the photographs
that were never taken,
beneath veneers never applied,
like a ghost silently pacing marble halls
sensed but unrecognised.

Spinning Plates

I saw a man spinning plates
- large white plates on anorexic sticks
swaying as if troubled by an irresistible breeze -
and marvelled at his dexterity,
how he managed to defy gravity
wearing black trousers and a white smile.

In the muffled introduction I had missed his name
and the echo of foreignness about it.
Or was it the distraction of "his Beautiful Assistant",
her name absorbed not by applause
but rather the mesmerising prospect of seeing
her magnificent breasts pop tremulously
from the feeble guard of her sequinned gown?

The show had been uninspiring
- the way free things often are -
and I had debated the wisdom of staying.
But before I could move,
before I could encourage my corpulent neighbour
(fat with over-indulgence in low-quality popcorn)
to release me to the aisle,
we were both invisibly trapped -
by the unnamed Artiste's benign smile
and his Accomplice's voluptuous bosoms.

Stella (her name revealed as he called her forwards;
every man in the crowd thinking "Bend down! Bend down!")
bore a stack of white plates on a cheap plastic tray,
her smile less certain than his.
And then, as swiftly as we focussed on Stella,

four men arrived to deposit the thin rods
(three poles each) unannounced and virtually unseen.
I caught a whisper to my right:
"This isn't 'The Melodic Marcello', is it?".
Unlikely; not with twelve poles and a pile of china plates.

Taking a plate - almost lifting it from the tray
with the power of his smile alone - he placed his free hand
on the nearest pole and bent it, almost double.
There was a thin gasp - someone fearing a 'crack!'
and splintering wood - and he smiled, then raised the plate.
From somewhere a feeble drum roll,
and then it was away, the first plate,
spinning about its axis,
swaying on the unstable yet resolute pole.
And from the back of the squalid hall
a ripple of applause.

There was no time to draw breath.
Plate after plate, Stella's burden became transferred
to the willowy posts; two, three, four, five.
At six the first plate began to wobble,
but with a flick of his wrist on the pole
its rotation was restored
- seven eight, nine (back to two, three, four)
ten, eleven, twelve!
A crescendo.

My corpulent companion seemed to have mislaid
all sense of mundane reality,
his enthusiasm bent on a collision course with apoplexy.
Again and again the plates feigned collapse;
again and again they would be rescued

as he caressed the poles, nudging, encouraging,
smiling his plate-white smile.
It looked easy. Like juggling.
And I thought: "We all juggle. Daily.
Living our lives is a performance worthy of the stage.
Keeping things in the air; spinning, airborne.
No drum roll. No applause. No Stella."

And then - one by one - he removed the plates
from the poles and asked for volunteers.

I may have been half-way from my seat
(on my way out perhaps)
when the applause started.
I may have been poked in the ribs, or suddenly
- and inexplicably - had a pin shoved into my arse.
Who knows?
But in a moment, Stella was guiding me
(my eyes fixed on her glorious cleavage)
across the threshold from floor to stage.
He smiled at me as if he had read my mind
("Easy, is it?")
then offered the first plate.

I looked up. There was no more applause.
The audience had thinned.
Even the fat man had returned to his popcorn.

He started me off;
and as his hand guided mine
to get a feel for the pole,
my mind raced on: "I didn't ask for this!".

At first the plate fell.
He caught it. We tried again.
It fell. It was caught.
After six attempts it spun.
There was something unconvincing in its movement
- like a learner reversing around his first corner -
but once it was going,
once I could feel the plate's rotation,
feel the pole as it rocked in my palm, I smiled.

Then he span a second plate.

Abandoning the first - even for a moment - brought fear.
But then, remarkably, there were two plates spinning.
I found I could manage. I was in control. I smiled.

Then he span a third plate.

The plates rocked, uneasily, uncooperatively.
I jiggled the poles, trying to cajole them as effortlessly
as he had done. I fought gravity.
The weight of the plates increased,
the poles became hard to move.
I began to panic.

Then he smiled.
And looking at me, he slipped his hand
inside the front of Stella's gown, and said:
"Easy, isn't it?".

Then they were gone.
And still the plates rocked,
spinning unevenly, defying physics.

It was as if there had never been centrifugal force,
or gyroscopes, or Isaac Newton.
It was as if there had only ever been heavy white plates
balancing on inadequate white poles.
Even the fat man began to boo,
spitting popcorn from the back row.

And I thought "I didn't ask for this!",
caught between the fear of leaving
and the dread of breaking crockery.

The Aridity of a Wasteland

The last stunted olive trees stand
sharp-edged under a chill desert sun as
stony cornfields fade into the native badlands.
Any outward grandeur is concealed by turbulence;
at the edge of a village of cinder block houses
drivers sell bananas and buy scrap metal.

Interrupted by war, invasion and uprisings,
and lacking the status of the powerful old families
to keep his slippery grip on power,
he was forced to weave creativity and cruelty
into a daring and blood-stained career
- and live for months in blackest depression.

In landscapes where he felt most at home,
he gave with kingly generosity,
his idealism and high-minded courage
portrayed not in words but in stone:
minarets spiked the hills all around,
and garden plots gathered in neat defensive ovals where
splashing water created an atmosphere of peace and tranquility.

The most serious miscarriage of his lifetime
may have been been a hostile biographer
who denied there was one mind behind it all.

His hat down low against the slicing wind,
thin lips set in a taut straight line,
he was forced to create his own monument;
a towering memorial of snowy stonework,
finely sculpted objects in hard pink limestone,

a soaring high-peaked roof steeple-sharp.
In ways that challenge the modern imagination,
he was trying and discarding theories about identity,
and tackling a vast puzzle in four dimensions.

Some of those who should remember him would
re-bury his bones and seal them in concrete.

Invasion

The public face for several years
        (the spawn of politics)
was a policy of denial about everything
        (the spawn of war).
In the growing dark underbelly
        (the spawn of commerce),
a Money Man's operation was
        to process cash for secret dealings,
        to formalise some kind of treaty,
        to mitigate the overwhelming fear when invaders got near.

Economic crashes were Trojan Horse events.

Not always in one piece any more,
there are Veterans willing to come forward
        (veterans of politics, of war, of commerce)
and recall the actual things that did happen.

"How did all of this begin?"

        "It was almost like a wave, a vacuum, a break in the air."

Sea Traders

Lost to the great waves of the sea
                    and now beached in mythology,
a continent was supposed to have existed
                    that surpassed all others,
its capital established by law
                    against the sublime aspect of
a bay that ran toward the south.
                    As if predestined,
the name for the waters between
                    the port and the open seas
was associated with serpents.

A long history of navigation finds
                    in salt-caked and failing volumes
inscriptions concerning their voyages;
                    the privations of the journey,
the delicacy of their constitutions,
                    and their sufferings from
hunger on the way.

The shores of the mainland always seemed closer;
to the Merchants who traded for her at sea
and those who would have played the spy.

Empiricism

Curved by matter,
starlight is deflected as it passes
the variations of a pendulum;
the attraction of positive to positive
is the medium that carries light
and gravity the force binding
objects that are not really solid.

Regardless of the name,
       a theory must apply equally,
       must connect and unify,
and avoiding creative dissonance,
       conform to the four rules of philosophy.

Four Books, Five Classics

Messengers of a superior civilisation
ignored the lessons of history -
a complex and fascinating product
of colonial expansion and civil war -
to feed the heroic victories that define
a nation's image of itself.

A timeless culture of foreign invasion
begat this resistance-driven narrative
and riding on a wave of peasant hunger,
offered control over the unwieldy country.
Yet stability remained illusive as they
rebuilt the empire via a mix of persuasion and force.
New notions of law, time and space
were motors for change and modernisation,
and acceleration of the Civil Service,
offered an attractive storyboard for Nationalists
rational to the point of obsession,
disappointed to discover modernity
is not an all-or-nothing phenomenon.

The Superiority of Nature

Trapped as an unintentional consequence
                of the weather's sudden shift,
the mist of myth envelops the moors
                and strands us in
a bleak backdrop of gothic literature and Hollywood.

It is not merely our innocence
                whipped by gale-force gusts of change.
National identity balances on the tip
                of some vast unstable scree,
the trip wire of ownership
                sweeping through the country in lines
we are told are defined by
                long-held tensions over class
and philosophical clashes with those
                who regard nature as a commodity
and live in listed buildings stripped down
                to hardwood floors and wainscoted walls.

The veteran Naturalist, still boasting
                a mind that crackles like a generator,
embraces a neutral landscape
                rich with the smell of fresh air,
and revels in the magic of
                a bird's nest the colour of winter.

Mirage

The past is a mirage, untouchable, distant;
a romantic myth born from a need to believe in something
and that what we have done matters.

You stand, boots ankle-deep in sand,
dune shapes shifting, promising beauty, delivering deception;
and from this fluid vantage point
a speck or two of green stands out,
a glimpse of palm trees teasing in the haze.
And is that the reflection of the blazing sun
on the watery skin of an oasis?
Your realise your thirst as your mind plays tricks with distance,
and the oasis seems a memory reflecting more than light,
an image of what you once were.

Are those the trees beneath which you sat toasting a future,
champagne in fluted glasses,
the bubbles making you all laugh, imbibing gaiety?
How can it have been,
for this is a perpetually revising vista on which you stand;
an inconstant perspective from which to view
that which purports to be your future
yet is simply your past to come.

Others have tried to fix their place
in these inhospitable climes.
Capturing the sands and turning them to inadequate brick,
they have built outwards and upwards;
drawn images of trees, the oasis' sunlight,
and framed these secure within their personal monuments.
Now if you look - if anyone looks -

you can see their memorials rising
high against a rippling horizon,
imagination the only key
to open doors to what might yet lay inside.

Lacking the pyramid builders' craft,
you stutter towards your own monument
creating an edifice from the things
you have to hand; a photograph perhaps,
the snapshot of a mirage.

And all the while I too build.
My sand is made from words,
words that shift and move,
that fall silent through my fingers,
that blind me when the mood is dark
and everything is become invisible.

Accent

Speak to me in a lilted accent
     filled with Mediterranean promise,
          electric like the brush of your hair on my arm.
Let your lazy vowels caress me
     as I lay my hand against the small of your back
          and have my fingers trace your perfect spine
               upwards, unobstructed.
Teach me the nuances of your tongue,
     demonstrate its fluency
          perfecting cadence and divine inflections.

And if you cannot speak to me
     as you stand across the road
     or stroll into a store
     or laugh with your friends as you lounge in the park,
          then forgive me if I imagine that one day
          you might utter a few simple words,
          heavenly transport to me.

Poetry

An unruly tobacco-stained beard
hides a dashing gilded-age adventurer
who lost everything through gambling
and ignoring the cautions of men
uncomfortable with uncertainty.

Men who have been stranded
taking their chances crossing the desert,
were willing to expose themselves to risk
on perilous journeys into the unknown,
braving the soul-crushing loneliness of travelling
to seek out and learn new things.

Theirs is a landmark attempt to navigate,
difficult explorations into unmapped territories
to probe unlit labyrinths knowing
their choices might lead to negative outcomes.

Unable to leave the quest unfinished,
they set out once again, dreaming of wider horizons,
the trails taken and not taken,
striving for legendary images to cast a spell over the reader.

About 'Human Archaeology' and Ian Gouge

If there is a unifying theme running through 'Human Archaeology' it is the relationship between Man and his history, memory, and how looking back at the past - at both its events and its artefacts - gives us the context for who we are.

This reflection manifests itself in a number of ways. In poems such as "Ripples" or "Beyond the Boundary" we look back into history in a traditional, narrative way. Far from being idealised, however, experiences are never far from disappointment, especially when it comes to journeying - as in "The Grand Tour", "Exploration", or "Northwest Passage" - where we see reality jar with hope or expectation.

If such viewpoints might be regarded as 'romantic' then we shouldn't be surprised as there is romance in this volume too. However, this is also often unsatisfying because the outcomes are not ones of fulfilment ("Rose"), or have only generated disappointment or confusion ("The Dissemblance of Rock"), or are decidedly *un*-romantic ("Standing in Doorways", "Love-locked").

That the two strands - history and romance - are linked also runs through many of the pieces, and nowhere more explicitly than in "Abstraction" which opens with "Romance is an overlay on reality", and elsewhere is the assertion that what we view as 'history' is simply a romantic interpretation of the past: "a romantic myth born from a need to believe in something / and that what we have done matters" ("Mirage"). More significantly perhaps, is the notion that true history cannot be known: "True history resides in all the photographs / that were never taken, / beneath veneers never applied, / like a ghost silently pacing marble halls / sensed but unrecognised" ("Abstraction").

Whether this undermines the thrust of the poems that focus on the fabric of history - perhaps most evident in the "Archaeology" poems themselves (I, II, III and IV) - is a moot point. Perhaps it serves only to highlight just how difficult and complex the relationship between us and our history actually is.

That real conflict is an ever-present in our past - and in personal lives - is echoed too in poems such as "Days of Tea and Backgammon", "Reading the Runes", and "War Artist", and where there is such conflict there will always be a fight for justice and liberty. In some respects, the poet - whilst keeping a safe distance from much of the debate, acting primarily as overseer and interpreter - is as much a rebel as those who appear in pieces such as "The Revolutionary", "Assassination" or "Uprising". And perhaps sharing some of their ideals, in one or two instances - most noticeably "The Permanence of Shrapnel" and "Camouflage" - the author lets his guard down in an attempt, ultimately in vain, to locate himself within his own history.

❊

Although Ian Gouge has been writing for many years, he still suffers from that common complaint felt by all writers at one time or another - namely, the nagging uncertainty around the quality and relevance of their work. 'Human Archaeology' is his first collection of new poetry since 'Second Sight' (pub. 2013). His 'Collected Poems (1979-2016)' (pub. 2017) takes its material from a significantly broader period.

The themes and preoccupations of 'Human Archaeology' crystallised as the new poems began to gather themselves into something approaching a coherent whole. The examination of history and its artefacts is probably a wholly appropriate subject given that some of the pieces were crafted from 'found' material - much in the same way perhaps as an Archaeologist assembles and then displays fragments found through their excavations.

All Ian's books are available via the Internet and through a small number of traditional outlets - a number that will hopefully grow during 2017 and beyond.

www.ingramcontent.com/pod-product-compliance
Lightning Source LLC
Chambersburg PA
CBHW021335060726
47591CB00006B/2023